Fundamental
BASKETBALL

Coach Jim Klinzing, Coach Mike
Klinzing, and the following athletes
were photographed for this book:
  Rob Byrne,
  Cara Cashin,
  Carnel Edwards,
  Tim Helms,
  Chris Hull,
  Beth James,
  Jackie Kosmider,
  Kate Kozub,
  Ray Logan,
  Josh Morgan,
  Allison Pender,
  Amy Picard,
  Theresa Roach.

Fundamental
BASKETBALL

Jim Klinzing and Mike Klinzing
Photographs by David Kyle and Andy King

Lerner Publications Company ● Minneapolis

The Fundamental Sports series was conceptualized by editor Julie Jensen, designed by graphic artist Michael Tacheny, and composed on a Macintosh computer by Sean Todd. The Fundamental Sports series was designed in conjunction with the Beginning Sports series to offer young athletes a basic understanding of various sports at two reading levels.

Photo Acknowledgments
Photographs on pp. 4-5, 6, 16 (right), 18, 19, 20, 21, 22, 24, 25, 26, 27, 30, 32, 33, 34 (right), 35, 38, 39, 40, 41, 43, 44, 46, 47, 48, 49 (middle and bottom), 50, 51 (left), 53, 54, 55, 56, 58, 59 (left), 60, 62 (left), 64, 65, 67, 72, by David Liam Kyle. Photographs on pp. 2-3, 12, 28, 29, 31, 36, 37, 49 (top), 51 (right), 61 (left), 62 (right), 63, 69, by Andy King.

Other photographs reproduced with the permission of: p. 7, University of Kansas Athletic Department; pp. 8, 9, Naismith Memorial Basketball Hall of Fame; p. 10 (bottom), 11 (left), Bettmann Archives; pp. 10 (top), 66 (top right), Robert Tringali Jr./Sports-Chrome East/West; pp. 11 (center and right), 17, 23, 59 (right), 66 (bottom), Brian Drake/SportsChrome East/West; p. 13, AP/Wide World; pp. 16 (left), 61 (right), Vincent Manniello/SportsChrome East/West; p. 34 (left), © PVA/Sports 'n Spokes, photo by Curt Beamer; p. 66 (top left), David L. Johnson/Sports-Chrome East/West.

Diagrams by Laura Westlund.

Library of Congress Cataloging-in-Publication Data

Klinzing, James E.
    Fundamental basketball / Jim Klinzing and Mike Klinzing ; photographs by David Kyle and Andy King.
      p.   cm. — (Fundamental sports)
    Includes bibliographical references (p.   ) and index.
    Summary : An introduction to the history and techniques of basketball.
    ISBN 0–8225–3458–4 (alk. paper)
    1. Basketball—Juvenile literature. 2. Basketball—History—Juvenile literature. [1. Basketball.] I. Klinzing, Mike. II. Kyle, David (David Liam), ill. III. King, Andy, ill. IV. Title. V. Series.
GV885.1.K54 1996
796.323—dc20   95–44817

Manufactured in the United States of America
2 3 4 5 6 7 – JR – 04 03 02 01 00 99

Contents

Chapter 1

HOW THIS GAME GOT STARTED

Deadly accurate shooting, graceful jumping, no-look passes, and swarming defenses are all part of the game of basketball. But James Naismith, the inventor of basketball, would be shocked to see how his game is played today. On a December day in 1891, his goal was to create a game that would be fun and challenging for his class of young men at the YMCA Training School in Springfield, Massachusetts. He never could have imagined that someday millions of players all over the world would play his game.

Years after inventing the game, Naismith said, "I had in mind the tall, agile, graceful and expert athlete. One who could reach, jump, and act quickly and easily." When you read these words, which of today's basketball stars come to mind?

Great players seem to score with ease. They move with lightning quickness. Fantastic dribbling and passing are common in almost every game. The best players hustle on defense throughout the game.

James Naismith developed the game of basketball while teaching in Massachusetts. He later taught at the University of Kansas, where this photograph was taken.

7

THE FIRST GAME

This illustration of the new game of basketball was drawn in 1892 by a student at Springfield College. The drawing was printed in the student newspaper.

The Early Years

Naismith's first game certainly did not resemble this description. There were nine players on each team. Players could not **dribble** the ball, and they could not jump while shooting. There wasn't even a basketball. Instead, Naismith's players used a soccer ball and two peach baskets suspended on a balcony 10 feet off the floor. A custodian removed the ball from the basket after a score. *Basketball* was the obvious name for the game.

When the ball went out of bounds, the players made a mad dash after it because the first team to touch the ball got it. Baskets counted for one point. Players were not awarded a **free throw** after a **foul,** but three team fouls resulted in a point for the other team.

After the young men in that YMCA class graduated, they spread the game rapidly across the country. The first women's game was played in Springfield, in March of 1892. The Minnesota State School of Agriculture beat Hamline University 9-3 in the first men's college game, which was played in 1895.

Metal hoops replaced peach baskets as goals in 1893. The **bank shot** became possible in 1895 when backboards were added. But it was 1913 before the out-of-bounds rule was permanently changed to award the ball to the opponents of the team touching the ball last. Players gradually began to dribble to advance the ball upcourt instead of always passing to each other.

Several significant rule changes were made in the 1930s. The team with the ball was required to advance the ball

Naismith, on the right in the center row, coached this group of young men in his new game—basketball. This team, which played in the winter of 1891-92, was the first basketball team.

beyond the center court line within 10 seconds. The three-second **free throw lane** rule was added to prevent tall players from standing under the hoop to score easy baskets. Before 1937 there was a center jump after every basket. Teams with tall centers had an advantage in regaining possession of the ball even after their own team scored. This rule change better balanced the competition, sped up the game, and greatly increased scoring.

Professional Basketball

The first league to pay its players was the National Basketball League, which was formed in 1898. It lasted just two years. Other pro leagues tried and failed. Another National Basketball League (NBL) was created in 1937. Most of the teams in this league were in midwestern cities. The Basketball Association of America (BAA) began play

in 1946. The teams in the BAA were mostly on the East Coast. The NBL and BAA merged in 1949 to form the National Basketball Association (NBA). A rival league, the American Basketball Association, began in 1967, but it was absorbed by the NBA in 1976.

Around the World

Basketball has truly been a world game for more than a half century. The first Olympic basketball games were played in Berlin in 1936. The American men's team won every gold medal until 1972. That year in Munich, Germany, a controversial end to the game resulted in the Soviet Union team winning the gold. The American players have not accepted their silver medals to this day. They truly felt they had won the game.

Again in 1988 the American team did not win the gold medal. The United States had sent a team of collegiate

The women's basketball team of the United States won the gold in the 1984, 1988, and 1996 Olympics.

Michael Jordan and the Dream Team won the men's basketball gold in 1992 and 1996.

all-stars to the Olympics, while many other countries fielded teams of older, professional players. American basketball officials decided to play by the same rules in 1992. The Dream Team was created. Magic Johnson, Larry Bird, and Michael Jordan were joined by nine other NBA stars including Charles Barkley, David Robinson, Patrick Ewing, and Scottie Pippen.

That team beat each of its Olympic opponents easily. The U.S. victories left little doubt that the best players in the United States were also the best players in the world. Players all over the world are getting better. There are now dozens of foreign basketball players in the NBA. One of the best known stars is Hakeem Olajuwon, who was born in Nigeria.

Boys and girls all over the world are practicing because they love this game and want to be the best. You can also become a very good player and help to maintain the tradition of great basketball at all levels of competition.

Great Big Men

George Mikan was the game's first dominant big man. He led DePaul University to national prominence in his college days. He later sparked the Minneapolis Lakers to four National Basketball Association titles. Mikan led the NBA in scoring in the league's first year with 27.4 points per game. He is a member of the Basketball Hall of Fame.

The Boston Celtics were the dominant team of professional basketball in the 1950s and '60s. Bill Russell was a 6-foot-10-inch Celtic rookie in 1956. In his first season, he led the Celtics to the NBA championship. After losing to Bob Pettit and the St. Louis Hawks the next season, the Celtics won eight straight championships. During these years, Russell had many classic battles with another outstanding big man, 7-foot-1-inch Wilt "The Stilt" Chamberlain. Chamberlain was the only player to score 100 points in a game. Can you believe that he averaged 50 points per game for an entire season? He was truly the greatest scorer in the game.

While the Celtics dominated the NBA, the UCLA Bruins won 10 college titles in 12 years. The Bruins won their first title in 1964 with no player in the starting five taller than 6 feet 5 inches. After winning again the next year, a 7-foot-2-inch freshman named Lew Alcindor arrived. Coach John Wooden was excited. In Alcindor's first varsity game, he scored 56 points. He went on to lead the Bruins to three straight championships. Later Alcindor changed his name to Kareem Abdul-Jabbar. He became the NBA all-time career scoring leader. He scored more than 35,000 points in his NBA career!

Two current great big men are Hakeem Olajuwon and Shaquille O'Neal. Hakeem led the Houston Rockets to two straight NBA titles and was the MVP in each of these playoff series. Hakeem has offensive moves that are catlike quick and deadly accurate. Shaq is big and strong. He dunks often and with great power. When he improves his shooting at the free throw line and at mid-range distances, he will likely lead his team to many titles.

Bill Russell

Kareem Abdul-Jabbar

Shaquille O'Neal

Chapter 2

BASICS

The goal of basketball is to score more points than your opponent. That means your team must be able to score when you have the ball on offense and play strong defense when your opponent has the ball. To play this great game, you need to understand the basic rules and moves.

The Court

You can practice basketball almost anywhere. A playground, driveway, alley, or even a basement can be a good place to practice. When you play on an organized team, the games will be played on a regulation court. The diagram on the next page shows the size and markings of a regulation court at the high school level. Many basketball courts are smaller because of limited space. These smaller courts are fine, especially for practice.

No matter how large the court, the free throw line is always 15 feet from the front of the backboard. The width of the free throw lane, sometimes called the paint, is 12 feet for most levels of play,

Rebecca Lobo led her team, the University of Connecticut Huskies, to an undefeated season and the NCAA women's college basketball championship in 1995.

13

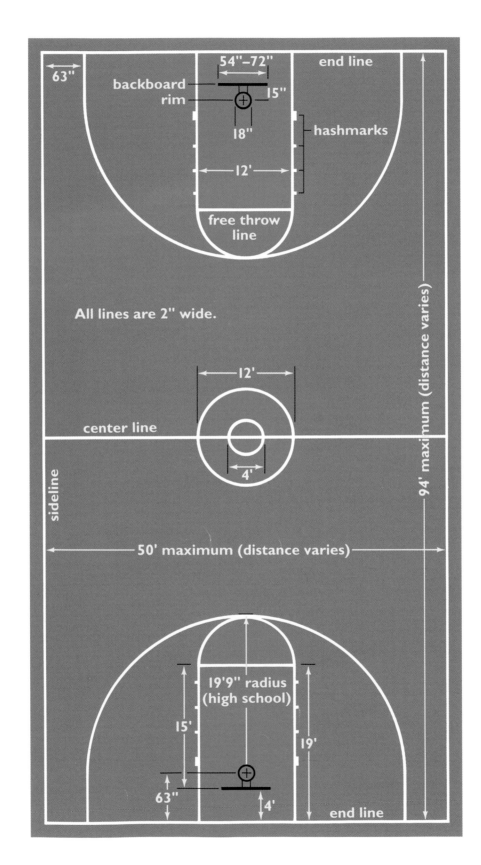

The Court

but 16 feet in the NBA. The three-point distance is 19 feet 9 inches for high school and college, 20 feet 6 inches in international play, and 22 feet for the pros. Regardless of the three-point distance, you should practice shooting from distances where you can make at least one of every three shots.

The official height of the basket (from floor to rim) is 10 feet. Professional players use a 10-foot basket. These players are almost all between 6 and 7 feet tall and very strong. You should use a basket height that is suited to your height. This will allow you to master proper shooting form. If your family puts a basket on the driveway, try to buy one with adjustable heights. As you become taller, you can raise the basket. The following is a guide for the proper basket height.

Rectangular Backboard

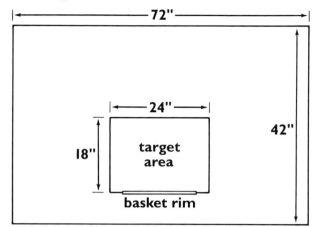

Fan-Shaped Backboard

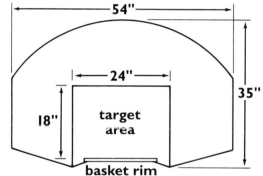

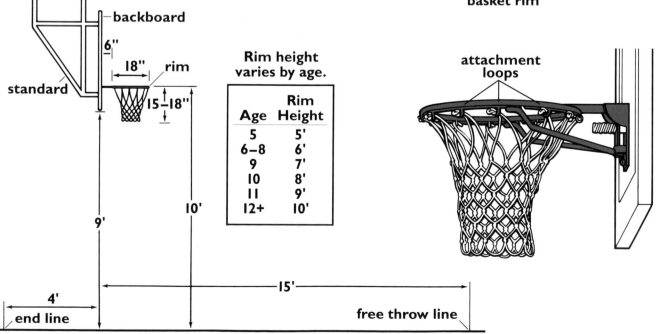

Rim height varies by age.

Age	Rim Height
5	5'
6–8	6'
9	7'
10	8'
11	9'
12+	10'

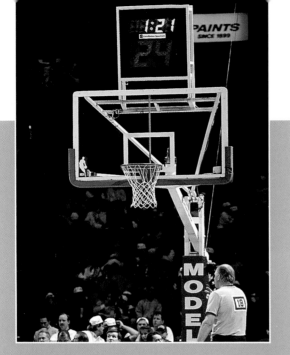

The Shot Clock

The National Basketball Association introduced the shot clock into basketball during the 1954-55 season. A team has 24 seconds to take a shot. Two clocks, one above each basket, keep track of the time, starting when a team takes control of the ball. If a shot bounces off the rim, the clocks are restarted at 24 seconds. If a team doesn't take a shot that scores or hits the rim within the 24 seconds, a buzzer sounds and the defending team gets the ball.

Games at the high school level and for younger players do not use a shot clock. Women's college and international basketball games have a 30-second shot clock. In men's college basketball, the shot clock is 35 seconds.

The shot clock was added to increase the speed of the game and prevent stalling. Basketball can be very boring when a team seldom tries to score. Coaches sometimes will have their teams stall when they are playing against a much better team. The strategy is to perhaps get a few lucky baskets and play great defense to stop the opponents. Once in a while it works, but not often.

The shot clock forces a team to make quick decisions and attack the basket. Players learn to take a good shot when it's available. If they wait too long, the defense may not allow another good shot. Defensive players know they won't have to chase the other team for a long period, so they can play aggressively for a brief time.

Equipment

A men's basketball measures 30 inches around. The ball used for girls' and women's basketball is 28.5 inches in diameter. The smaller ball gives players with smaller hands better control. You should buy a basketball made from material that is suited to what you can afford and where you play. Rubber basketballs are the least expensive kind. They are designed for outdoor play, but they can also be used indoors. An artificial leather ball is made for indoor and outdoor play. The best kind of ball is made of leather and is for indoor use only. High school, college, and pro teams use a leather ball.

The most important item of equipment for a basketball player is a good pair of shoes. The running and jumping in basketball causes a lot of pounding on the legs and feet. Thick-soled shoes absorb the shocks well. Shoes can cost $30-$100, so look for sales! The rest of your practice uniform can be a T-shirt and shorts or sweatpants.

Basketballs are most often orange or brown. A basketball weighs about 20 ounces and has a pebble-grain covering.

Positions

Five players are on the court for each team during a game. The center is usually the tallest player and plays close to the basket. The best centers can **rebound** well. They are skilled at scoring close to the basket.

A team will have two forwards. One forward is often called the power forward. This forward plays closer to the basket than the other forward. The power forward has many of the same skills as the center but is slightly shorter. The other forward, called a small forward, is expected to shoot well from longer distances. This player should also be quick at dribbling to the basket.

The point guard is typically the team's best ball handler. This player brings the ball upcourt, dribbles well, and passes the ball accurately. The point guard isn't usually expected to be a high scorer. The point guard controls the game and gets the ball to teammates so that they can score. The fifth player is the shooting guard. This is a player with good all-around skills. This player is a good ball handler, shooter, and passer.

Rules

A high school basketball game is divided into four eight-minute periods, or quarters. College games have just two 20-minute halves. After the first two periods or the first half, there is a 10-minute rest period called halftime. Coaches often use this break to plan their strategy for the remainder of the game.

The game begins with a jump ball at the center of the court. The referee

Mugsy Bogues

Never Too Little

You have to be tall to be a good basketball player, right? Tyrone "Mugsy" Bogues doesn't think so. At 5 feet 4 inches, Mugsy has always been the littlest player on his team. But that has never stopped him. He knew he could be good and he practiced and worked hard to improve his skills. He became the starting guard for the Charlotte Hornets of the National Basketball Association. Why? Because he never listened to anyone saying he was too small. Mugsy believes in himself.

Anthony "Spud" Webb is 5 feet 7 inches tall. He has played in the NBA for more than 10 years and was a starter many seasons. At his height he certainly can't jump very high, right? Don't tell that to the 1986 NBA Slam Dunk Champion or any of the millions of people who saw his fantastic display of dunking ability. He is also a great passer and can sink his shot. In other words, he has mastered the skills of the game. Don't let anyone tell you that you are too small. Practice, play, and prove them wrong.

tosses the ball up between two players, one from each team. These players are usually the centers. Each player jumps and attempts to tap the ball to a teammate. The team that gets the ball has gained the first possession. This will be the only jump ball of the game. After this jump, the alternate possession rule is used. Any time there is a held ball—where players from opposing teams both grasp the ball and try to pull it away—the ball is awarded to the teams on an alternate basis. Teams also alternate possession of the ball at the start of each of the last three periods.

Some of the rules for professional play are different. NBA games have 12-minute quarters. When there is a held ball, the two players jump. The team that wins the opening tip also gets the ball at the start of the fourth quarter.

Violations

Once you start dribbling, you may only dribble with one hand at a time. If you touch the ball with both hands at the same time, you must pass or take a shot. If you start to dribble again, you will be called for a **violation—double dribble.** Stopping your dribble and then starting to dribble again is also a double dribble violation. Another dribbling violation is carrying the ball. The dribbler's hand must stay on top of the ball. You cannot contact the ball on the side or the bottom and carry the ball.

Traveling occurs when a player moves both feet while holding the ball. When you hold the ball, one foot must be stationary. That foot is your pivot foot, and you cannot move this foot unless you are dribbling. However, you can rotate on your pivot foot while your other foot steps in any direction.

A team has 10 seconds to move the ball past the midcourt line. Once past this center line, a team may not allow the ball to go into the **backcourt** unless a player for the other team touched the ball last. The three-second rule means the team with the ball may not have any player in the free throw lane for more than three seconds.

After one team scores, the other team throws the ball in bounds from underneath the basket. The player passing the ball into play may move along the baseline as long as he or she stays behind the line. In every other out-of-bounds circumstance, the passer must keep one foot stationary. If the player doesn't, the other team gets the ball.

Fouls and Free Throws

Basketball players aren't supposed to push, pull, bump, or hit opponents. If you do these things, a foul should be called. How strictly these rules are enforced depends on the referees. Usually more contact is allowed in the pros and less is allowed at other levels.

When opposing players bump one another, the referee must decide which player ran into the other. The player who moved to the spot of the collision first is said to have had "position." The player who arrived second committed the foul. Did the defensive player bump into the offensive player or the other way around? A block is a foul on the defensive player and a charge is a foul on the offensive player.

Players at all levels are allowed five fouls before they are disqualified, or foul out. (The NBA allows players to have six fouls before they foul out.) A player who is fouled while shooting gets two free throws if the shot was missed, one if the shot was made.

If the player was not shooting when fouled, his or her team is given the ball out of bounds. In high school games, bonus free throws are awarded to a team when its opponents commit more than six fouls during one half of the game. The bonus means a nonshooting player who was fouled gets one free throw. If the player makes the free throw, he or she gets to shoot a second free throw. If the first free throw is missed, the ball is in play and both teams try to rebound the missed shot.

Two or three referees officiate a basketball game. The referees enforce the rules for fair play and are alert for

Technical Fouls

We've all seen them! An official's call goes against a player or coach, and suddenly they are jumping up and down, yelling at the official. Technical foul! Is it a coaching ploy? A moment of frustration? Or is it just a dumb play?

A referee calls a technical foul when a player or coach behaves inappropriately. This type of behavior includes fighting, throwing the ball at another player, arguing, or swearing. A technical foul is also called if a player is listed in the scorebook with the wrong number or name. If your team is given a technical foul, a player from the other team gets to shoot two free throws. Then the other team gets the ball. That's a potential five-point play for the opponents. Giving your competition five points can cost your team a victory. Keep your emotions under control and play smart.

violations. When one team commits a violation, the referee stops play. The referee gives the team that was fouled a free throw or the ball, depending on the situation.

Scoring

Free throws are worth one point. Any shot other than a free throw is called a **field goal.** All field goals that are made inside the three-point line are two-pointers. Whether a shot is a **layup, dunk,** or long **jump shot,** the basket counts two points. For a three-point basket, the shooter releases the ball while both feet are behind the three-point arc.

Now that you know the basic rules, get your ball and practice. Soon you will be ready for games on the driveway, playground, basketball camp, or at school.

Chapter 3

SKILLS

Basketball is thrilling to watch and play. For you to be successful as a basketball player, you must master the fundamental skills of the game. Scottie Pippen, Hakeem Olajuwon, Anfernee Hardaway, and other great players have mastered the skills of shooting, passing, dribbling, rebounding, and defense. How can you master these skills too? Perfect practice and more perfect practice!

Shooting

The main goal of basketball is to score more points than the opponent. Putting the ball into the basket is, therefore, the most important skill in basketball. Most players love to practice their shooting. All it takes is a basketball, a hoop, and effort.

There are three types of shots every player needs to develop: a **set shot**, a jump shot, and a layup. When you practice these shots, remember the letters **B-E-E-F + C.** Each letter stands for an element of correct shooting form.

Hakeem Olajuwon was a big reason the Houston Rockets won back-to-back NBA championships in 1994 and 1995.

The **B** stands for *balance*. As Allison shoots, her feet are slightly wider than shoulder width apart. Her knees are bent enough to let her spring off the court, and her weight is balanced. When Allison has good balance, she rarely misses her shot.

The first **E** stands for *elbow in*. Allison brings the ball to chest level on her shooting-hand side. Her elbow is directly under the ball. Allison's arm forms a 90-degree angle. By keeping her elbow in, Allison keeps her shot in line with the basket.

The second **E** stands for *eyes on target*. Allison looks at the front of the rim closest to her shooting position. She has the habit of always watching that spot when she shoots. Her goal is to push the ball just over that spot on the rim and into the basket.

The **F** stands for *follow through*. As the ball leaves Allison's hand, her elbow straightens and the ball rolls off her fingertips. The ball never touches the palm of her shooting hand. Allison snaps her wrist after releasing the ball just as if she were reaching into the cookie jar for a chocolate chip cookie.

The **C** stands for *concentration*. This is the most important part of shooting. Allison doesn't worry about the defenders, the crowd, or the referees. All she thinks about is the ball going into the basket. The ability to concentrate separates great shooters from good shooters. You can be a great shooter by remembering **B-E-E-F + C**, the main ingredients of any shooting menu.

● *Set Shot*

The set shot is used most often at the free throw line. Allison places her shooting hand on the back of the ball and her guide hand at the side. As the shot is released, Allison rises up on her toes.

The key to being a great free throw shooter is practice and concentration. Allison has developed a routine she uses before every free throw. Her routine relaxes her and it helps her to make the shot. Many players bounce the ball a couple of times and take a deep breath before shooting.

● *Jump Shot*

The jump shot is the most common shot taken in basketball. The only difference between the jump shot and the set shot is that the shooter's feet leave the floor when he or she shoots a jump shot.

Beth remembers B-E-E-F + C when she takes a jump shot. She releases the ball at the top of her jump, before she starts coming down. This allows her to have all her power behind the ball. Beth releases the ball from above her head. She doesn't have to jump as high as she can, just high enough to shoot over her defender.

● *Layup*

The layup is a shot taken when approaching the basket on the dribble. When shooting a layup from the right side of the basket, the player's right hand is behind the ball and the left hand is at the side, to guide the shot. The right knee comes up as if it were attached by a string to the right elbow.

Carnel jumps off his left foot and aims the ball for the corner of the square on the backboard. The shooting form is the exact opposite for a left handed layup, which is taken from the left side of the basket. Always practice layups at game speed, so that you will be ready when defenders try to stop you from scoring in a game.

The final skill of a great shooter is knowing when to shoot. No one likes to play with a ball hog. Shoot when you are open and you have the best opportunity to score. When playing, take only the shots that you have a good chance of making. Otherwise, pass the ball to a teammate who is in a better position to score than you are.

Passing

What's the best way to get open shots? Good passing! Being a good passer means giving the ball to your teammates when they are open. If you follow that simple rule, your coaches and teammates will love you.

The quickest way to advance the ball up the floor is by passing. Don't believe it? Challenge a friend to a race. Pass the ball to someone at the other end of the court, while your friend dribbles another ball. See who wins!

When you pass the ball, be sure your teammate can catch it. Don't try to throw a bullet pass when a softer pass is needed. If a teammate has the ball, be ready and able to catch passes. Always have your hands open and your eyes on the ball at the offensive end of the floor. You will be ready for any pass.

● Chest Pass

Throw a **chest pass** with two hands and release the ball at chest level. Kate's hands are on either side of the ball with her thumbs pointing toward each other. As she releases the ball, she steps toward the receiver and snaps her wrists. She finishes with her thumbs pointing down.

● *Bounce Pass*

The **bounce pass** uses the same fundamentals as the chest pass. Ray starts
with both hands on the ball and follows
through with his thumbs down. He steps
toward his receiver, aiming for a spot
on the floor about two-thirds of the way
to that player. The ball should bounce
once on the floor and the receiver
should catch the ball at waist level.

● *Push Pass*

The **push pass** can be thrown with or without a bounce. Instead of using both hands, Chris uses one hand to push the ball. The other hand is at the side of the ball to guide it. Chris follows through toward the receiver with a wrist snap just like that used for a jump shot.

● *Overhead Pass*

To throw an **overhead pass,** Tim grips the ball in the same way that he does for a chest pass or bounce pass. With both hands on the ball, Tim takes the ball above his head, brings his arms forward, and snaps both wrists while stepping toward the receiver. He aims for the receiver's chin so his teammate doesn't have to lunge to catch the ball.

When you have learned the fundamentals of these passes, the best way to practice passing is to get out and play in pickup games. The more games you play, the better you will react with good passes. Remember, make the simple pass to your open teammate and you'll be on your way to being a great passer.

Basketball on Wheels

Basketball can be enjoyed by players of all skill levels and abilities. Wheelchair basketball is growing throughout the United States. Playing the game in wheelchairs allows players with a variety of lower limb disabilities to test their talent against others with similar disabilities.

The main technique to be mastered in wheelchair basketball is the ability to maneuver the chair through traffic. Wheelchair basketball players are allowed two pushes of the chair between dribbles. How well a player can maneuver the wheelchair and still control the ball most often determines victory. Standard basketball rules apply in most situations, including violations, fouls, free throws, and out-of-bounds plays.

Many NBA teams sponsor wheelchair teams. These teams play other wheelchair teams and participate in tournaments. They also take on teams of able-bodied players who play in wheelchairs. The wheelchair athletes usually win by a wide margin!

How about basketball on in-line skates? Yes, it is being played! If you've mastered in-line skating, give it a try. The slam dunk may be a real adventure in this game, so be careful!

Dribbling

Every player should be able to dribble the ball well with either hand. However, dribbling should usually be your last option when you receive the ball. You should first try to pass or shoot before you think about dribbling. There are two situations in a game that require different types of dribbles.

● Speed Dribble

Advance the ball quickly up the court with a **speed dribble.** Allison pushes the ball out in front of her body with the ends of her fingers as she runs to keep up with the ball. She keeps her head up and doesn't look at the ball so that she can see her teammates when they break open to receive a pass.

● *Control Dribble*

When closely guarded, Beth uses a
control dribble. She flexes her knees
and protects the ball by keeping her
body between the ball and the defender. Beth keeps the dribble low to
have better ball control. Again, she
keeps her head up and uses her fingers
to control the ball.

Rebounding

Leaping high, grabbing a missed shot, and making the pass to start a **fast break** is an exciting part of playing basketball. Next to shooting, rebounding is probably the most important skill in basketball. What makes a great rebounder? It's simple—effort and desire! Assume every shot is a miss and get into position to get a rebound.

● *Defensive Rebounding*

The key to defensive rebounding is **boxing out** your opponent. Carnel keeps Ray from the ball by putting his body between Ray and the basket. Carnel faces the basket and his back-side touches Ray. Carnel has a wide stance, with his arms out and hands up. After the boxout, he leaps as high as possible to get the ball after it caroms off the rim.

● *Offensive Rebounding*

Pulling down an offensive rebound means getting to the ball despite the efforts of your opponents to keep it away from you. Hustle, make every attempt to move around your opponent, and jump for the rebound.

To get around the player boxing out, step left or right or spin off that player in either direction. You can also fake as though you were going to move in one direction and then go the other way.

Offensive rebounding is hard, but you will feel fantastic when you pull down the missed shot and put the ball back up and into the basket for two points.

Defense

Players often forget that half of the game is spent playing defense. Don't neglect the defensive end of the court as a player or you may never have the opportunity to reach your dreams. Every player can be a good defender. It takes strong desire! Do you have it?

Jackie is in the basic defensive stance with her feet spread more than shoulder width apart. She bends her knees as if she were about to sit down. Her head is up so she can concentrate on her opponent and her hands are out to each side to deflect passes. Notice that her back is straight. She is ready to play defense.

When an opponent has the ball, Allison concentrates on that player's belly button area. Sometimes a player will fake with her head or arms. But a person's belly button goes where the player goes. As her opponent dribbles, Allison moves sideways without touching her feet together. She doesn't run or cross her feet. She slides, keeping her body between the offensive player and the basket. When an opponent changes direction, Allison will step backward with the foot that is nearest to where the opponent is going. She continues her defensive slide.

When you do a good job of guarding a player with the ball, you will soon be guarding a player without the ball. Your stance remains the same, but raise your hands slightly higher to disrupt any potential passes. You don't need to follow your opponent everywhere he or she goes on the court. If the player you are guarding is on the side of the court opposite the ball (the help side) you can stay near the middle of the court. From the middle, you will be prepared to help any of your teammates if they get beat. This move, shown on the next page, is called help and recover. Help your teammate, then recover to guard your opponent.

3–2 Zone Defense

2–3 Zone Defense

● *Player-to-Player and Zone Defenses*

Teams use either a **player-to-player defense** or a **zone defense.** In a player-to-player defense, you are responsible for guarding your opponent and preventing that player from scoring. A zone defense requires that each player protect a specific area of the court. When the ball enters your area, you guard the opponent who has the ball. Zone defenses aren't allowed in professional basketball.

Player-to-player defense is used when a team has five good defensive players. These players are quick, and they hustle to stop their opponents from penetrating to the basket for easy shots. This defense is hard work, but once players have mastered the fundamentals of defensive play, this is the most effective defense. You will have great pride when you have prevented your opponents from getting easy baskets.

Why would you use a zone defense? Slower teams benefit when using the zone because players don't have to cover the entire defensive end of the court. This reduces the advantage the faster team may have.

A zone defense is also good when the opponents have one particular strength. Zone defenses are labeled with numbers that correspond to the alignment of the defensive players, starting at midcourt and moving toward the basket being defended. Against a good outside shooting team, a coach might use a 3-2 zone to strengthen the team's outside defense. A 2-3 zone places two defensive players outside and three near the basket. This defense is used against teams with good inside scorers, because it gives the defense an inside rebounding advantage.

Good defense requires that all five players work together to stop the other team. Everyone must help and recover. Next time you play, concentrate on developing your defensive skills. Coaches will appreciate your efforts, and you will love being able to stop your opponent from scoring.

To become a complete basketball player, you must master all the skills of the game. The next chapter gives instruction in how to practice. If you play and practice correctly, you will become the best player you can be.

Chapter 4

PLAY AND PRACTICE

Eric leaps high to grab the defensive rebound. He makes a chest pass to Mike, who speed dribbles upcourt using the middle lane. Ernest and Tucker are on either side of Mike. Who will get the pass? Mike reaches the free throw line, looks left, but bounce passes right to Ernest, who lays the ball on the glass for a layup. The ball rolls across the rim, but it doesn't drop in. Shawn, trailing the fast break, leaps high and lays the ball in the basket. Wow! What a play by Shawn. That was real hustle to get two points. And he's fouled!

Shawn goes to the line for one free throw. He bounces the ball twice, eyes the basket, and smoothly strokes in the shot to complete the three-point play. The Mustangs drop back on defense.

Ernest's man has the ball and takes a jumper from 10 feet. The Mustangs boxout for the rebound. The ball caroms off the rim. Shawn jumps and snares the ball. Right now this team is really playing at both ends of the court. The Mustangs will be tough to beat tonight. Their fans are giving them a standing ovation.

Joining a Youth League

If you aren't old enough for interscholastic competition, think about joining a youth basketball league. It's a great way to have fun and meet new friends. To find a league, contact the local recreation department, the high school athletic department, or look for notices in the sports section of the newspaper.

A youth league should emphasize participation and the fundamentals of basketball. A young player starting out needs to learn new skills and try them out against players of similar ability. Coaches should emphasize teaching fundamentals to all players while providing plenty of fun activities. Avoid coaches who only want to win, yell at their players, or don't provide every player the chance to play and practice.

How do you learn to play this well? Playing in pickup games on the driveway, at the local park, or at school is a great way to improve your basketball savvy and skills. Play in pickup games as often as possible. Try to play against players who are better than you, to challenge yourself. This is how you improve!

When you find yourself playing against less talented players, work on your weaknesses. For example, you may want to only dribble with your left hand or work on your passing. Work on a specific skill every time you play and you'll be excited by the improvement you make.

Basketball is a team game. Do your best to be a team player, but remember to work on your individual skills as well. The best players will earn most of the playing time. Coaches choose the players they think will help the team be most successful. Your goal is to become the most talented player you can be through preparation and good practice habits. Can you do it? Of course you can!

Practicing

One of the great things about basketball is that you can practice alone. Not having a practice partner is no excuse for a basketball player. Of course, it's more fun to practice with friends. However, your friends may not have the desire to practice as often or as hard as you do.

If you are on a school team, you will have regular practices during the season. Your coach will plan these sessions. During the off-season, you will be responsible for practice. Find a place to practice. It may be the driveway, playground, street, school gym, or recreation center. It may even be your basement. Practice sessions should include the following drills.

● Ballhandling Drills

Mastering ballhandling drills can be both challenging and fun. As you get better, try to do them faster. Do each of these ballhandling drills for about 30 to 60 seconds. Even if these drills are difficult at first, stick with them. Watch other good players and you'll get ideas for many additional drills. Soon you will be handling the ball like a pro.

● **Body circles:** Josh and Jackie circle the ball around their bodies. They start at waist level, progress up to the head, and gradually move down to the ankles, circling one leg at a time. First they move the ball in one direction, then the other.

● **Figure 8s:** Chris and Amy stand with their feet spread slightly wider than shoulder width apart. They move the ball in a figure-8 pattern between their legs. Then they repeat the drill, moving the ball the other direction. They can also do this drill by using a low dribble in a figure 8 around and through their legs.

● **Tipping:** Tipping the ball back and forth from hand to hand is one of Kate's favorite drills. She uses the ends of her fingers while moving the ball from her ankles to over her head.

● **Figure 8 high dribble and carry:** While standing upright with his feet spread slightly wider than shoulder width apart, Chris dribbles the ball once backward through his legs and catches it in his other hand behind him. He then swings his hand and ball forward around his body at waist level. He bounces the ball once backward between his legs and catches it with the first hand. He also reverses the drill, with the dribble moving the ball forward through his legs.

● *Dribbling*

Work on various types of dribbling as you move around the practice area. Remember to work with both hands equally. Keep your head up and your eyes forward. Don't look at the ball as you dribble. Here are some drills.

● **Dribble in place:** Dribble with one hand, then alternate hands, and then dribble with your eyes closed.

● **Speed dribble and layups:** Dribble the length of the court. When you approach the free-throw line, quickly cut to the basket to shoot a layup.

● **Dribble in a zigzag pattern up and down the court:** Use your change-of-direction dribble to move downcourt.

● **Crossover dribble:** While in a good dribbling position with the leg opposite your dribbling hand forward, dribble three times. Then quickly dribble the ball across your body to the other hand while stepping forward with the opposite leg.

● **Dribble up and down the court:** Cara, in the photo below, uses a speed dribble from baseline to baseline.

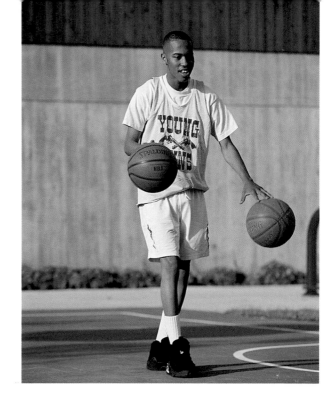

● **Dribble two balls while standing or running:** Can you dribble two balls like Carnel is doing in the photo above?

● **Change-of-pace dribble:** Josh dribbles up and down the court, varying his speed and direction and changing hands, in the photo above.

● *Shooting*

Everyone loves to shoot and score, but remember to practice all the skills. Reward yourself with shooting practice after you've worked on your ballhandling and dribbling. The most important shots to practice are layups, set shots, free throws, and jump shots. Stay close enough to the basket so that you use correct shooting form.

Remember to use B-E-E-F + C: Keep your balance, elbow in under the ball, eyes on the rim, follow through, and concentrate only on the ball going through the basket.

● **Layups:** Allison, at left, does at least 20 layups with each hand. Be sure to practice from both sides of the basket.

● **Free throws:** *Make* a minimum of 50 free throws during every practice. Remember to develop a routine you can use for every free throw.

● **Three-point shots:** Are you able to maintain good shooting form? Then shoot 25 three-pointers in practice. If not, wait until you are bigger and stronger to develop your three-point shot.

● **Set shots:** Tim, above, starts three feet from the basket. He takes 10 shots from there, and then moves to another spot. He takes a total of 50 shots.

● **Jump shots:** To practice jump shots, Ray, at right, starts close to the side of the basket. He uses the backboard and takes 10 shots. He then moves around the court, taking more shots. He will use a variety of moves and one dribble before shooting after stepping to the right, left, or forward. Ray shoots at least 50 jump shots.

Practice Schedule

Practice at least three times a week for about one hour. That will be easy during the summer. You'll have plenty of time. Also, whenever you have a chance to play, do it. What is a good practice session? Here goes:

Skill	Minutes
Ballhandling	*5 minutes*
Shooting	*15 minutes*
Passing	*5 minutes*
Rebounding	*5 minutes*
Shooting	*5 minutes*
Defense	*5 minutes*
Shooting	*15 minutes*
Ballhandling	*5 minutes*

Tips:
- *Perform a variety of drills for each skill.*
- *Challenge yourself to improve each day.*
- *Practice with other players when possible.*
- *Practice with better players to test each other.*
- *Keep a positive attitude on days when practice is not going well.*

Once school is back in session, you may not have as much time. Your school work will always be your number one priority. But you still can probably find an hour a day for basketball. Right after school is a great time. Use your driveway when the weather is good, or if you live near a court, go there. When the weather turns cold, use your basement to dribble, ball handle, and pass. Watch out for the light fixtures!

Conditioning

You will really improve as a basketball player as you practice daily. With this improvement in skill, you will be matched against better players and teams. Such factors as strength, endurance, quickness, speed, jumping ability, and agility often determine the best players. In a game of equally skilled players, the better-conditioned team will win. You want to be the best-conditioned player.

Basketball players need to be strong to jump high for rebounds. Endurance allows players to hustle the entire game. Speed, quickness, and agility will improve scoring moves and are needed to play tough defense. You will develop outstanding fitness for basketball by conditioning three days per week. Alternate weight training workouts with jumping and running workouts.

● *Weight Training*

The best way to become stronger is to train with weights. However, if you are a beginner, find a knowledgeable coach to help you. Weight training can cause injuries when performed improperly. Each exercise must be done with perfect form.

Basketball players benefit from exercises such as bench press, seated leg press, lat bar pulldown, knee extension, knee curl, two-arm curl, forward dumbbell raise, toe raise, triceps extension, and wrist curls. Ask your physical education teacher or coach to recommend a facility where you can lift safely.

● *Jumping*

Higher jumping will improve your shooting and rebounding. Warm up with rope skipping. Start with 100 jumps. Use any style. In fact, try to learn as many different ways to jump rope as possible. The variety will develop your coordination. Challenge yourself and make it fun.

Next, do jumping exercises on a soft surface like grass or gym mats. Don't jump on concrete or asphalt. These hard surfaces can hurt your legs. After exercising, rest about one minute. The following exercises will get you jumping higher and farther.

● **One step and vertical jump:** Take a quick step forward and jump as high as possible. Repeat the drill by stepping with the other foot. Do 10 jumps on each leg.

● **In-place jumps:** Rapidly jumping back and forth across a line improves quickness. Jump forward, backward, and from side to side. Start jumping with both feet and progress to using just one foot. Do 10 jumps.

• **Vertical jumps:** Energetically throw your arms up into the air with each jump. Immediately upon landing, jump again. Perform 10 jumps.

• **Skipping for height:** Swing your arms vigorously to gain maximum height on each skip. Skip 20 times.

Slowly, over several weeks, increase your total jumps from 100 to 200 in each workout. Do this by adding sets of these exercises, or by adding exercises your coach recommends. Don't rush your progress. Remember to rest about one minute between each exercise. With rest, you can do your best on every drill.

● *Running*

You will be a better basketball player when you can run for long periods with speed and endurance. After jumping, run. You will run your best when you use good form. Keep your head level and steady. Your arms should swing forward and backward without causing your shoulders or trunk to rotate. Keep your trunk upright with a slight forward lean. Lift your knees high when sprinting. Your feet should point straight forward. Land on the balls of your feet when sprinting. Land softly on your heels when running more slowly. Proper running form will allow you to run faster with no added energy cost. It will also reduce your chances of being injured.

Start by running for about 12 minutes. Add one or two minutes to the time for each run. After six weeks, you should be running 24 minutes. If you must walk a little at first, that's okay. Learn the pace you are able to run nonstop. You shouldn't be exhausted by these runs. If you are, slow down.

Once you have the endurance to run nonstop for 24 minutes, work on adding speed and quickness. This is accomplished with short sprints and quick starts. Sprint on a soft surface like grass.

Run 6 to 12 sprints in each workout. These sprints should be between 20 and 40 yards long. In the beginning, your sprints should be shorter. Gradually sprint farther. Walk slowly back to the start after each sprint. The rest is important. It allows you to sprint at top speed. Eventually you should plan a variety of different sprint workouts to challenge yourself and to keep these workouts interesting.

Practice at least one hour three days a week. Weight train, jump, or run on the other days of the week. Your improvement on the basketball court will be amazing. Don't wait—start today.

Chapter 5

RAZZLE DAZZLE

You will be excited by your improved play. Others will notice how much better you have become in all aspects of the game. They may not know how hard you have worked in practice and during games. They may not realize how much effort you put into your conditioning. That's okay! You know the secret of success.

You may now be ready to step up your game and become one of the best players in your area. Here is a sampling of skills to practice that will take your game to new heights.

Shots

To become a real scoring threat, you will want to master a variety of shots. Your skill and flair will make defenders struggle to keep you from putting big numbers into the scorebook.

Picking a Camp

Summer basketball camps are a great way to learn more about playing the game. You will get a chance to play with other good players and meet many new friends. There are two types of camps: overnight and day.

Overnight camps are most often held at colleges. Campers sleep in the college dormitories and eat in the cafeteria.

Day camps are held at colleges or local high schools. Some day camps also offer half days. These camps will run three or four hours a day for a week. That's plenty of basketball without overdoing it. More experienced players will want to attend all-day camps. These camps can provide plenty of high-level instruction and competition.

A good camp emphasizes plenty of action and the fundamentals. Try to attend a camp with players who are as good or better than you are. This will challenge you to work hard and improve your game. You don't want to attend a camp where you sit around.

Who is teaching at the camp? Instructors who have experience working with young basketball players will often do a better job than big-name coaches or players who have little or no experience working with kids.

Camp should always be a good experience and have plenty of enjoyable activities. Contests and games that give each camper an opportunity to win and be successful contribute to the quality of the camp.

● *Underhand Layup*

The **underhand layup,** or finger-roll layup, is used by tall, strong players to give them an advantage over their shorter defenders. The same fundamentals are performed as for the regular layup, except that the ball is laid softly up to the backboard with an underhand flick of the wrist.

● *Hook Shots*

Tall players who play near the basket use the **hook shot** and the **jump hook shot**. Your body protects the shot from being blocked as you release the shot with one hand. Your shooting hand sweeps outward and upward from the side of your body. The follow-through extends your arm over your head.

The hook shot, shown above, is taken with a one-footed takeoff from the foot closest to the basket. The jump hook, shown on the next page, is taken from a two-footed takeoff.

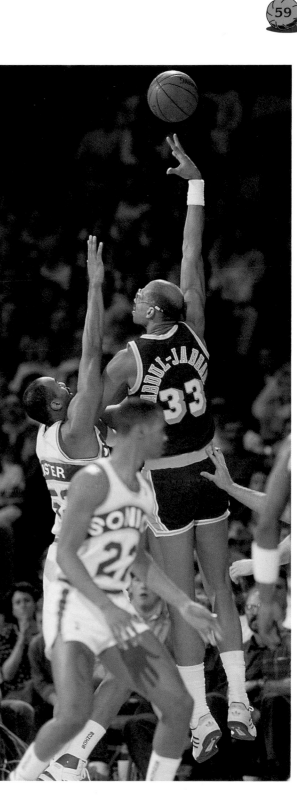

The hook shot used by Kareem Abdul-Jabbar is nicknamed the "skyhook." Abdul-Jabbar's shot seemed to come out of the sky, because he is 7 feet 2 inches tall.

● *Three-Point Shot*

The three-point shot has really changed the game of basketball. It has become an important part of most teams' offenses. Once you have developed proper shooting form and have the strength to maintain that form from three-point land, you should begin practicing three-point shots. At first, your threes will resemble a set shot taken with a forward jump toward the basket. As you gain experience, your jump will be more upward than forward.

The key to being a good three-point shooter is knowing when to take the shot. The three-pointer is often most effective after the ball has been passed inside and come back out to an open shooter behind the line.

● *Dunk*

What is the most exciting shot in basketball? You're right—the dunk! All of us wish we could fly through the air like Michael Jordan, but reality says most of us can't. If you have jumping ability, the fundamentals are the same as for a layup. When you get above the rim, simply throw the ball forcefully down with one or two hands. If you can really sky, add your own creative flair to your dunks by shifting the ball or your body while in the air.

Shaquille O'Neal's thundering dunks have made him a favorite with fans throughout the country and around the world.

Offensive Moves

Not only do you want to be able to score with every type of shot, but you also want to get free from your defender to take open shots. Quickness, clever ball handling, and mastering the following moves will dazzle the opposition.

● *Triple-Threat Position*

The triple-threat position is taken by an offensive player who has the ball. Rob, below, has his knees flexed, his head up, and the ball in both hands at waist level. In this triple-threat position, he can dribble, pass, or shoot. Rob can also fake any of these moves. Every time you receive the ball in scoring position, you should immediately get into the triple-threat position.

● *Crossover Dribble*

A well-executed crossover dribble crosses up opponents, leaving them to wonder how you bolted past them so fast. This offensive move is used by great NBA ball handlers such as Mark Price, Kevin Johnson, and Tim Hardaway. When you perform this move correctly, you won't have to worry about your defender for a while.

In the photos above and on the next page, Ray shows this move. He starts dribbling to the right. Then he plants his right foot and quickly makes a low dribble to the left hand while shifting direction to the left. The move can also be executed in the opposite direction.

Ray starts his dribble going to his right, then shifts his weight and switches the ball to his left hand. His defender, Carnel, can't switch directions fast enough to stay with Ray.

● *Screens*

Setting a **screen** is a useful skill that is often overlooked by young players and coaches. A screen allows a teammate to get open for an easy shot. Don't ignore screens. Below, Allison sets a screen by positioning herself in the path of a defender. This allows Cara to elude her defender and break free.

● *Baseball Pass*

The baseball pass is actually thrown more like a football pass. It is a long, downcourt pass used for a fast break or to break through a pressing full-court defense. Tim moves the ball behind his ear with both hands and then fires a long pass by extending his passing arm forward. Accuracy is the most important aspect of throwing the baseball pass. Remember, the best pass is a completed one.

Magic Johnson

Michael Jordan

Larry Bird

Who was the Greatest?

Earvin "Magic" Johnson, Larry Bird, and Michael Jordan ignited NBA thrills during the 1980s and early '90s. Each had a great college career, was an all-American, and played in the NCAA Championship. As good as they were in college, each really blossomed in the pros.

Magic was 6 feet 9 inches. He played point guard as no one had before. He was a great passer and dribbler. He retired at the start of the 1991–92 NBA season because he had the virus that causes AIDS. He returned to the Los Angeles Lakers late in the 1995–1996 season. He played until the team was defeated in the playoffs, then he retired again.

Bird, at 6 feet 9 inches, dominated from the forward position. Passing and shooting were his best skills. Like all great players, Larry wanted the ball in his hands as the game clock wound down.

Jordan could do it all at 6 feet 6 inches. No one has ever displayed such individual creativity in moves to the basket. He was unstoppable when he decided a basket was needed for the Chicago Bulls. Jordan won seven straight scoring titles. Unbelievable! All basketball fans were saddened by Michael's sudden retirement in 1993 after the Bulls won their third NBA title. Fans were ecstatic when he returned in 1995 and led the Bulls to three more titles. Michael decided to retire a second time in January 1999.

● Fast Break

A fast break is simply a way to move the ball quickly upcourt by passing and dribbling. This gives the offensive team a chance to score before the defense can retreat and stop the shot. Magic Johnson and the Lakers often scored on layups because they grabbed a defensive rebound, got the ball to Magic, and then hustled up the court.

The players on the fast break sprint to spread out across the floor. This makes it more difficult for the defense to stop the ball. With accurate passing, a fast break often ends in an easy layup. When a player like Shawn Kemp receives the final pass, the play ends with a *wham-bam-slam* dunk and the fans go wild.

Everyone dreams of being a great basketball player. The skills and ideas presented in this book will give you a solid base upon which to build your basketball career. No one can take away your goal. Live it, believe it, and, most importantly, practice for it. You will love what happens.

BASKETBALL TALK

backcourt: The half of the court with the basket one's team is defending.

bank shot: A shot that is intended to gently hit the backboard and fall through the basket.

bounce pass: A pass that bounces between the passer and the receiver.

boxing out: A move to establish a position close to the basket while rebounding. A player faces the basket and spreads his or her feet to block an opponent's path to the basket.

chest pass: A pass that is thrown with two hands, starting at chest height.

control dribble: A method of moving the ball with low bounces while keeping one's body between the opponent and the ball.

double dribble: A violation in which the player with the ball dribbles with both hands at the same time. A double dribble violation is also called if a player dribbles, holds the ball, and then starts dribbling again.

dribble: A continuous bouncing of the ball on the floor, using one hand.

dunk: To slam the ball through the basket from above the rim.

fast break: A quick movement of the ball downcourt by passing or dribbling, in an attempt to score before the opposing team can set up its defense.

field goal: A shot that is scored while the ball is in play. A field goal is worth two points unless it is taken from beyond the three-point arc, in which case it is worth three points.

foul: An illegal act that involves physical contact with an opponent.

free throw: A chance to shoot at the basket without interference from an opponent. A free throw is awarded because of a foul by an opponent. The shot is taken from the free throw line and is worth one point if it's made.

free throw lane: A 12- or 16-foot-wide portion of the court underneath each basket, between the end line of the court and the free throw line. Because these areas are often painted a different color than the rest of the court, they are often referred to as "the paint."

hook shot: A shot in which the shooter begins with his or her back to the basket, then pivots and sweeps the ball up and over his or her head with one hand.

jump hook shot: A hook shot during which the shooter jumps off both feet before releasing the ball.

jump shot: A shot in which the shooter jumps and releases the ball at the peak of his or her jump.

layup: A shot in which the shooter dribbles toward the basket, jumps, and gently bounces the ball off the backboard and into the basket.

Ray practices his dunk.

overhead pass: A two-handed pass that starts above the passer's head.

player-to-player defense: A style of defensive play in which each player is assigned to guard a specific player on the other team.

push pass: A pass that is thrown with one hand pushing the ball and the other hand guiding it.

rebound: To gain possession of the ball after a missed shot. An offensive rebound is a rebound by the shooting team. A defensive rebound is a rebound by the defending team.

screen: A move by an offensive player to legally block a defender's path so that the offensive player's teammate can get free for a shot or pass.

set shot: A shot that is released while both of the shooter's feet remain on the court.

speed dribble: A method of moving the ball with a high bounce while running quickly.

traveling: A violation in which the player with the ball moves both feet without bouncing the ball.

underhand layup: A layup in which the shooter's hand is palm up when the ball is released, so that the ball gently rolls off the fingers and into the basket. Also called a finger-roll layup.

violation: An illegal act that doesn't involve contact with another player.

zone defense: A style of defensive play in which each player is assigned to defend a specific area, or zone, of the court.

FURTHER READING

Anderson, Dave. *The Story of Basketball*. New York: William Morrow and Company, Inc., 1988.

Bird, Larry with John Bischoff. *Bird on Basketball*. Reading, Mass.: Addison-Wesley Publishing Company, Inc., 1985.

Gutman, Bill. *The Pictorial History of Basketball*. New York: Gallery Books, 1988.

Jacobs, A.G. *Basketball Rules in Pictures*. New York: The Putnam Publishing Group, 1989.

Klinzing, Jim and Mike Klinzing. *Basketball for Starters and Stars*. Benton, Wis.: Syskos Basketball Books and Videos, 1995.

Pruitt, Jim. *Play Better Basketball*. Chicago: Contemporary Books, Inc., 1982.

Scott, John W. *Step-By-Step Basketball Fundamentals for the Player and Coach*. Englewood Cliffs, N.J.: Prentice Hall, 1985.

Vancil, Mark. *NBA Basketball Basics*. New York: Sterling Publishing Company, Inc., 1995.

FOR MORE INFORMATION

Amateur Athletic Union of the
United States
Walt Disney World Resorts
P.O. Box 10,000
Lake Buena Vista, FL 32830-1000
www.aausports.org

Basketball Congress International
1210 E. Indian School Road
Phoenix, AZ 85014

National Basketball Association
645 Fifth Avenue
New York, NY 10022
www.nba.com

National Collegiate Athletic
Association
6201 College Blvd.
Overland Park, KS 66211-2422
www.ncaa.org

National Wheelchair Basketball
Association
110 Seaton Building
University of Kentucky
Lexington, KY 40506
www.nwba.org

USA Basketball
5465 Mark Dabling Blvd.
Colorado Springs, CO 80918-3842
www.usabasketball.org

Youth Basketball of America, Inc.
P.O. Box 3067
Orlando, FL 32821

INDEX